David Hermon Van Hoosear

A Complete Copy of the Inscriptions Found on the

Monuments

David Hermon Van Hoosear

A Complete Copy of the Inscriptions Found on the Monuments

ISBN/EAN: 9783337399122

Printed in Europe, USA, Canada, Australia, Japan

Cover: Foto ©ninafisch / pixelio.de

More available books at **www.hansebooks.com**

A COMPLETE COPY

OF THE

INSCRIPTIONS

FOUND ON THE

Monuments, Headstones, &c.

In the Oldest Cemetery

IN

NORWALK, CONN.

SEPTEMBER, 1892.

Dedicated to the Memory of Norwalk's First Ancestors

BY

DAVID H. VAN HOOSEAR,

WILTON, CONN.

(P. O. HURLBUTT STREET, CONN.)

BRIDGEPORT, CONN. :
THE STANDARD ASSOCIATION, PRINTERS.
1895.

THE Cemetery from which this copy was taken is situated at East Norwalk in the old village where the first settlement was made, Home lots laid out, and a few rods South-east of the site of the first Church, which was on the North corner of East Avenue and Fort Point Road. The Cemetery is triangular in shape, bounded on all sides by highways and enclosed by a picket fence. There are many graves seen which are unmarked by Headstones, and very many more of the early ancestors remains were deposited in this burial place, of which no mark or tradition is left. Here rests one of our Colonial Governors, (Gov. Thomas Fitch) No. 230. Probably the first minister Rev. Thomas Hanford is buried here, (tradition says near the headstone of his son Thomas,) where is seen a "flat Brown stone" the inscription is wholly obliterated. The 2d minister Rev. Stephen Buckingham, (No. 209) and 3d minister Rev. Moses Dickenson (No. 234) a tutor of Yale college. Buckingham St. John (No. 20), a son of the 1st Pastor, Rev. Jedeiah Buckingham. Two deacons; one of 1st church.

Five militia Capt., one militia Col., a Rev. Soldier, a Col., two Capt., and seven soldiers in late war who have inscribed stones, a Master of Arts, M. D., au eminent Dentist, and many whose title has never been chiseled on the stone marking their grave.

The yard contains but one vault; (The Raymond.) In summer the flowers placed in this cemetery by descendents of deceased friends show that the memory of the dead here are not forgotton. It is well cared for. May this interest continue, and the forefathers be allowed to rest and remain where they are. The object of the undertaking is to preserve definite memory of these early ancestors of Norwalk.

"He is a public benefactor who gathers together from the crumbling monuments and preserves in printed form the memorials erected by their cotemporaries over the early fathers of the country.".

[N. L. Collamer, Wash. D. C.]

The reader may say where are *our* Earliest Ancestors? To this the answer must be within the above enclosure. It is true over fifty years had passed after the settlement of the town before the first inscribed headstone appears, yet we have no record yet found, no tradition still kept or known of, or evidence of the existance of any other. This was for the first church in the heart of the ancient settlement. Imported stones were costly, and in a few Graveyards, stones from the field were selected, with the initials and year of death roughly chiseled upon them. A number appear in Stratfield Cemetery (now Bridgeport, Conn.,) before 1700, the earliest 1688 and one in Fairfield 1687. No well inscribed stone appear in either of these before 1700. From the above facts we are led to believe this is the first cemetery in Norwalk.

Each Stone is given a number commencing on the South side, and is copied in six sections between parallel lines from East to West so the small numbers are stones on the south part of the yard and so northward.

THE INSCRIPTIONS

IN THE

Cemetery at Norwalk, Conn.

As Copied in September, 1892, by David H. Van Hoosear, Wilton Conn.

1—Samuel W. Potter,
Died June 15, 1869, Æ. 80 y'rs 8 mo's & 7 days. Also, Sarah B. wife of Samuel W. Potter, Died April 1, 1864, Æ. 76 y'rs & 12 days.

Father.
2—Charles Dennis.
Born July 6, 1829. Died April 14, 1888. At Rest.

In Memory of
3—Wm. St. John.
Who died July, 1805, Æ 42 years.

In Memory of
4—Hannah, [St. John]
Relict of Wm. St. John, who died Nov. 21, 1810, Æ. 50 yrs.

5—James Andrew,
Died March 9, 1871, Æ. 66 y'rs 3 mo's & 19 days. Elizabeth, his wife, died Feb. 1, 1888, Æ. 76 y'rs & 5 mo's.

Mother.
6—Elizabeth, [Silcox]
Wife of William Silcox. Died March 7, 1890, Æ. 47 y'rs 4 days.

A light from our household is gone,
A voice we loved is stilled,
A place is vacant in our hearts
That can never be filled.

7—Delia, [.(St. John) Thorp]
Daughter of William and Hannah St. John, and wife of David B. Thorp; died June 11, 1845, aged 50 years, 6 months and 17 days.

In Memory of
8—Maria P. St. John.
Born May 18, 1794, Died December 9, 1873.

Here Lies Interred the Body of
9—William St. John, A. M.
Who departed this life Feb'ry 1st, 1800, in the 56th year of his age.

Tremendous death, how awful is thy sway,
Thy dreadfull Summons Mortals must obey;
In time of sacred ardor, seek the heavenly shore
Where joys forever bloom, and death shall be no more.

10—David Burr Thorp.
Born March 6, 1794. Died March 16, 1857, aged 63 years and 10 days.

11—Our Little Zaydee Thorp.

In Memory of
12—Matthew C. St. John,
Born March 16, 1792. Died May 9, 1856.

In memory of
13—Mary Esther St. John.
Who died April 15, 1850, Æ. 97 y'rs. 5 mo's. & 2 d's.

"Thou shalt come to thy grave in a full age, like a shock of corn cometh in his season."

[Brownstone.]
In Memory of
14—Mrs. Ann St. John,
Wife of Col. Stephen St. John, who departed this life April 28th, 1797, in her 64th year.

15—Morris Jennings.
Died Nov. 8, 1882, Æ. 58 yrs. 9
mo. and 9 d's.

Here lies interr'd the body of
16—Mr. Hooker St. John,
Who departed this life March
the 10th, 1782, in the 40th year
of his age.

All you who pass by may drop a tear
O'er one who was as now you are.
But now he's gone and paid ye debt
The lot of all both small and great.

In Memory of
17—Ellen St. John.
Who died Oct. 27, 1849, Æ. 10
y'rs. Coloured.

18—Edward F. Jennings.
Died Aug. 10, 1885, Æ. 36 y'rs,
9 mos, and 9 Ds. At Rest.

[Marble Tablet.]
—d the body of
19—S—phen St. John, Esq.,
and —of the 9th Regt. of Foot
—he State of Connecticut who
departed this —— May the 9th
1785, in the 50th year of his age.

Hark from the tombs a doleful sou—
——and the cry
——view the ground
——must shortly lie.

The Grave of
20—Buckingham St. John,
A. B., late Tutor of Yale College in New Haven who was
drowned in returning home on
the 4th of May, 1771 in the 26th
year of his age.

A youth adorned with strong men-
tal endowments, cultivated with
polite and usefull literature, but
a sudden gust plung'd him in
the sea Blasted our hopes and left
his friends his country and sci-
ence to bewail the Loss: And
learn the Vanity of depending on
fleeting dust.

[Slate.]
Here Lyes Buried ye Body of
21—Mr. Mathias Saint John.
Aged 37 years. Dec'd 1732.

[Captain Joseph St. John, s. of
Joseph and Sarah (Betts) St. John
and "probably" grandson of Mark
Sention was born Nov. 5th, 1705,
married Susannah —— who was
born 1709, d. Dec. 4, 1749, aged 40

yrs, 2 mo., and buried near Joseph's Tomb Table. Her inscription reads "ye wife of Capt. Joseph St. John." He died Sep.
(probably) 1756 or 1760, aged 53 or
57 yrs. His residence was where
now lives Wm. H. Earle, East av.
nearly opposite the Governor
Fitch place. He was a rich man
and large laud holder, and after
his death there was erected to his
memory a brownstone Tomb Table similar to the Governor Fitch.
Beyond the memory of those living the entire inscribed slate
which was placed in the top of
this table, was missing, and vari-
ous traditions and rumors have
been handed down of the cause of
its removal, whereabouts and dis-
appearance. The author has thor-
oughly traced these to establish
for whose memory this table was
erected. At last he has in his
hands a part of the original slate
which was found while excavating
a blind drain on the Wm. H.
Earle's place, 1893. The St. John
cost of arms is a shield, and the
upper third has two stars and the
motto is "Data Fata Secutus,"
The coat of arms engraved on the
broken slate (which exactly fits in
the socket for it in the tomb table) bears a part of this motto
("Data Fata ——") the "Secu-
tas" being broken off. A large
portion of the shield is seen.
What remains to be seen of the
inscription is as follows:]

"The Rema—
CAPt JOSEPH—
lies here waitin—
Resurrection of S—
He departed SEP. t—
Ætat. 5—

Hark mortals Hark what vol—
Comes echoing from—
O my dear friends be wise
While vital spirits animat—"

Here lies the body of
22—Mrs. Susannah St. John,
ye wife of Capt. Joseph St.
John, who died December ye 4,
1749, aged 40 years and 2
months.

She that lies at rest within this tomb
Had Rachels face and Leah's fruitfull
womb,
Abigail's wisdom, Lydia's faithfull
heart
With Martha's care we hope Mary's
better part.

[Slate.]
23—Sarah Saint John,
Dau'r to Mr. Joseph & Mrs.
Susannah Saint John, aged 7
years 4 mo & 12 Ds. Died April
18, 1741.

[Slate.]
Here lies Buried the Body of
24—*Mrs. Sarah St. John*,
Wife of Mr. Joseph St. John,
who departed this life Aug'st
26th 1755 in the 90th year of her
age.

[Slate.]
Here lyes Buried the Body of
25—*Mr. Nehemiah Rogers*,
Who departed this life May ye
30th, 1760, aged 42 years and 12
days.

[Slate.]
Here lyes Buried the Body of
26—*James Rogers, Esq.*,
Aged 58 years& 5 mo. De'd,
July ye 13th, 1733.

[Brownstone.]
Here lies the Body of
27—*Mrs. Freelove Rogers*,
Relict to Capt. James Rogers
Esqr, who died Jan'ry ye 26th,
1739, in ye 46th year of her age.

28—*Our Little Eddie*,
Died Feb. 18, 1873, Æ. 1 yr. 7
m's 8 da.

[Slate.]
Here lyes ye Body of
29—*Sarah Saint John*,
Daut to Joseph Saint John, aged
24 years. Dec'd Decr ye 23d 17—

In memory of
29a—*Job Bartram, Esq.*,
Who died July 19, 1813, Æ. 78.
—+—
29b—*Jane Bartram*,
+
Died Oct. 1, 1847, Æ. 33.

29c—*Henry S. [Bartram,]*
Born Feb. 5, 17. 1867.

Jennie G.,
Born Oct. 10, 1837. Died Dec.
14, 1875. Children of Charles
J. and Elizabeth G. Bartram.

30—*Arthur R. [Underhill,]*
Son of Charles H. & Alice E.
Underhill. Died Aug. 28, 1882,
Æ. 21 y'rs & 20 days.
He died trusting in Jesus.

In memory of
31—*Mr. Isaac Scudder*,
Who died March 5th, 1784, aged
78 years.

[Slate.]
32—*Ruth*,
—N—O—DS—7.

[Brownstone.]
Here lies buried the Body of
33—*Mr. Samuel Grumman*.
Who departed this life Aug. ye
21st, 1747, aged 53 years.

In memory of
34—*Mrs. Elizabeth Scudder*,
Relict of Mr. Isaac Scudder,
who died Aug. 21, 1798, aged
93 years.

Here lies ye Body of
35—*Mrs. Sarah Scuder*,
Wife to Mr. Isaac Scuder, aged
30 yrs., 8 ms., 11 dayes, Dec'd.

[Brownstone.]
In memory of
36—*Rebeckah Grumman*,
Wife of Samuel Grumman, who
died May 24th, 1790, in the 94th
year.

37—*Clara Christerisen*,
Died March 9, 1892, Æ. 23 y'rs,
7 mo's & 11 days.

38—*Baby Helene E. [Madden,]*
Daughter of Fred. H. and Susie
Madden, born Dec. 22, 1890,
died June 13, 1891.

[Brownstone.]
Here lies Buried the Body of
39—*Mrs. Lois Carter*,
Relect of Mr. Sam'l Carter, who
died January ye 12, 1752, in ye
82d year of her Age.

40—Betsey Marvin,
Widow of Allen Betts, died Jan.
29, 1882, Æ. 20 Yrs., 3 mo's &
19 Days.

Here lies Buried the Body of
41—Mr. John Gregory,
Dec'd January ye 18, 1751, in ye
75th year of his age.
[Brownstone.]

42—Seth Marvin,
Died July 6, 1836, Æ 85 y'rs
& 6 mo.

Hannah,
His wife, died Dec. 12, 1846,
Æ. 85 y'rs & 4 mos.

43—Eliza Ann [Gay],
Wife of Wm. Gay, died Mar.
25, 1835, Æ. 29 y'rs, 3 mo. &
11 d's.
He loved him because he first loved us.
—John, 11, 19.

44—Lucretia,
Wife of Wm. Gay, died May
26, 1852, Æ. 52 y'rs & 14 d's.
But I trusted in thee, O Lord, I said,
Thou art my God.—Ps., 31, 14.

45—William Gay,
Died March 4, 1864, Æ. 62 y'rs,
3 mo's & 1 Day.

[Brownstone.]
In memory of
46—Seth [Smith,]
Son of Hutton & Phebe Smith,
who died of the Small Pox,
Feb. 22, 1799, in the 14th year
of his age.

47—Isabell E. [Richards,]
Wife of Frank H. Richards,
died Dec. 9, 1879, Æ. 25 y'rs, 7
mo & 20 days.

[Brownstone.]
In memory of
48—Sally [Smith,]
Daughter of Hutton & Phebe
Smith, who died of the Small
Pox, March 2d, 1799, in the 17th
year of her age.

49—James H. Brush,
Died May 20, 1884, aged 33 y'rs,
4 mo's & 14 Days.
—:0:—
We shall meet beyond the river.

In memory of
50—John E. King,
A Mechanical Engineer, Died
Sept. 19, 1881, Æ. 36 y'rs.

51—Henry Marvin,
Died June 18, 1882, Æ. 84 yrs,
2 mo's & 15 Days.
"Who shall separate us from the love
of Christ?"

52—Harry [Youngs,]
Son of Washington & Susie
Youngs, died Dec. 2, 1881, Æ.
2 yrs., 10 mo's & 29 days.
Of such is the Kingdom of Heaven.

In memory of
53—Phebe [Smith,]
Wife of Hutton Smith, who
died June 4, 1836, Æ. 72 years.
How in an instant she is called,
Eternity to view;
No time to regulate her thought,
Nor bid her friends adieu.

54—Phebe E. [Marvin,]
Wife of Henry Marvin, died
Jan. 1, 1892, Æ. 89 y'rs, 2 mo's
& 1 Day.
The last enemy that shall be destroyed
is death.

55—Theresa J. [Marvin,]
Daughter of Henry & Phebe
E. Marvin, died April 24, 1845,
Æ. 2 years & 10 Days.

56—Charles F. [Lockwood,]
Died Feb. 20, 1871, Æ. 6 mo's
& 10 D's.

Stephen A.
Died Mar. 9, 1872, Æ. 2 mo. &
10 D's, children of C. M. &
M. F. Lockwood.
These lovely ones, so young and fair,
Call'd hence by earthly doom,
Just came to show how sweet flowers
In paradise would bloom.

57—Mattie [Goodwin,]
Daughter of William & Ann
Goodwin, born Mar. 4, 1873,
died Mar. 16, 1879.
She sleeps in Jesus.

In memory of
58 - Hannah [Smith,]
Wife of Founten Smith, who
died Aug. 8, 1824, aged 93 years.

In memory of
59—Hannah [Smith,]
Wife of James Smith, who
died Aug. 20, 1811, Æ. 57.

60—John Austin,
Born Aug. 16, 1798, died Sept.
4, 1872, aged 74 years & 18
Days.

61—William Goodwin,
Died Aug. 20, 1885. Æ. 52 yrs.
5th N. Y. Heavy Art'l.

Ann,
Wife of William Goodwin, Died
Feb. 7, 1892, Æ. 58 y'rs.

In memory of
62—James Smith,
Who died June 17, 1813, Æ. 57.
—+—

63—Mary Austin,
Wife of John Austin, died Aug.
5, 1882, aged 69 years.

"She hath done what she could."
—Mark, 14:8.

64—Nehemiah Ganung, Jr.,
Co. F, 1st N. Y. Eng.

65—Aaron Cook,
Died Nov. 19, 1873, aged 67
Y's. 6 m's & 18 Days.

A native of Lancaster, Mass.

[Slate.]
HERE lyes ye body of
66—Mr. Eliphalet Lockwood,
Jun'r, aged 28 years, 3
MONTHS & 24 Days, dec'd
October THE 17th, 1734.

[Brownstone.]
67—Mrs. Abigail Lockwood,

68—Jacob Wetzenstein,
Co. C, 75 Regt., N. Y. Vols.
died March 22, 1888.

69—Charles E. [Pitzer,]
Our Darling is Sleeping.
Son of Gustave & Augustine
Pitzer, born Sept 3, 1884, died
May 23, 1885.

70—Henry J. Brush.
Born. Jan. 15, 1816, Died June
20, 1884.

Vesta A.,
His wife, born Aug. 12, 1820,
died Apr'l 25, 1886.

[Slate.]
71—Ruth Belden,
Daughr of Lieut T John and
Ruth Belden aged. 14, years
died Jan'ry ye 21st 1704-5.

[Slate.]
—yes ye body of
72—Ruth INGOLDSY.
Died March ye 30 1729, in ye
23d year of her age.

73—Sarah F. [Allen,]
wife of Frank Allen Died Feb.
5, 1886. Æ. 50 yrs, 3 mos & 3
Ds.

At Rest.

[Brownstone.]
Here lies the body of
74—Peter [Hayes,]
Ye son of Isaac and Margaret
Hayes who died Nov'r ye 17,
1750 in ye 8 year of his age.

75—Alfred G. Corson
Died March 14, 1887, Æ—36 yrs.
2 mos. & 15 Ds.

At Rest.

Corson.

[Brownstone.]
76—Mr. Samuel Hayes.

[There is no No. 77]

78—Mary Mildred. [Corson]
Wife of Alfred D. Corson, Died
Dec. 10, 1883, Æ. 55 yrs 4 mos
& 26 D's.

Asleep in Jesus.

79 – *Freddie* [*Kaske*]

Died Nov. 2, 1874, age 9 mos.
& 20 Ds.

Charlie

Died Feb. 26. 1888, age 16 yrs.
& 24 Ds. Children of John
& Caroline Kaske.

Safe in the arms of Jesus.

[There is no No 80.]

81 – *Annie E.* [*Beers*]

Wife of Wm. H. Beers Died
O·t. 2. 1885. Æ 26 y'rs 5 mo's
& 11 D's.

Safe in the arms of Jesus.

82 – *Emeline* [*Merrills*]

Wife of Addison Merrills, Died
Mar. 20, 1882, Æ, 35 yrs, 8 mos,
& 20 days.

Dearest mother thou hast left us,
And thy loss we deeply feel;
But 'tis God who hast bereft us,
He can all our sorrows heal.

[Brownstone.]

In memory of

83 – *Deborah* [*Hanford*,]

Wife of Hezekiah Hanford,
who died Septr. 15th, 1803, in
the 78th year of her age.

[Hezekiah the son of No. 94 was buried
in this cemetery ; His headstone was
standing within the memory of some
living—but it is now absent. He was
buried next to his wife Deborah [No.
83]. He married Deborah Hayt dau
of Caleb Hayt Oct 7, 1743. He
served in the Coast Guards during
the Revolution. His children were:—

I. Daniel. b. June 26, 1744 Died April 12,
1797 [See No 86]
II. Deborah, b. Sep 26, 1746
III. Samuel, b Jan 7, 1748 d. July —.
IV. Hezekiah, b. July 24, 1753.
V. Mehitable, b. Oct 7, 1755, d. July —.
VI. Josiah, b. Dec 10, 1757, d. July. —.
VII. Lydia, b. May 27, 1759.
VIII. Elizabeth, b. Feb 27, 1762
IX. Grace, b. Oct 5, 1765 d. Mar 28, 1840
X. Susannah b. Oct 7, 1768.]

84 – *Joseph P. Hanford.*

Died Aug. 10, 1870, aged 88
years.

[Joseph Platt Hanford—[84] married
1st Charlotte St. John [See No 85].
Their children were:—
I. Daniel, who d. Sept 25, 1857.
Winfield Scott Hanford *his* son is buried
in Union Cem. Norwalk. His dau.
Mary, C. married Hon E. A. Woodward
of So Norwalk. Their child Lottie

Hanford Woodward is the 8th genera-
tion inclusive, of Wm and Mary
Haynes, [No 96] 5 generations of which
are buried in this cemetery.
II. Charles.
III. Winfield Scott.
Joseph Platt Hanford 2nd married Phebe
Northrop dau of Seth Raymond of
Wilton, Ct. [See No 88]. Their chil-
dren :
Joseph Platt Hanford b. March 8, 1818
Joseph P. senr. d. Aug 10, 1870.]

85 – *Charlotte* [*Hanford*]

wife of Joseph P. Hanford,
Died Feb, — 1816, Æ. 30 y'rs.

[Before marriage her name was Charlotte St. John. Sister to Chas. who
married Nancy Marvin dau of Matthew Jr.]

In memory of

85½ – *Daniel Hanford,*

who died April 12th, 1797 in
the 51st. year of his age.

86 – *Susannah* [*Hanford*]

Relict of Daniel Hanford, Died
March 10, 1836. Æ. 86 y'rs.

[Daniel Hanford. m. Jan 9—1773 Susannah Platt dau.of Capt. Joseph Platt,
she was born Jan. 4, 1750 d. Mar. 12
—1836. He was Capt. of Militia and
served in the active service for 3 mos
in the Revolution. His children
were:—
I. Edward, b. Mar 3. 1774.
II. Andrew, b. Aug. 18, 1775, d. Oct. 16, 1776.
III. Joseph. Platt, b. Aug. 23,1777, d. Sep. 18,
1778.
IV. Andrew, b. Dec. 9, 1779.
V. Joseph Platt, b. April 17. 1782 [See No
84].
VI. Deby, b. April.19. 1784.

[There is no No 87]

88 – *Phebe,*

Second wife of Joseph P. Hanford, Died May 26, 1860, Æ. 74
y'rs.

89 – *Elizabeth* [*Toby*]

wife of William T. Toby, Died
Oct. 17, 1872, aged 47'years,

Blessed are the dead who die in the Lord.

90 – *S. P. Ellwood*

Co. C 28th. Conn. INF.

[Slate.]

HERE Lyes ye Body of

91 – *Mrs. Mary Hanes*

Wife to Mr. William Hanes
aged 51 years Dec'd. July ye
22D. 1711.

92 —Edwin Barnes
Co. F 17, Regt, Conn. Vols,
Died Mar, 7. 1882.

[Brownstone]
In memory of
93 —Deacon David Comstock
who died Nov'r. 19th.1782 in the
62d. year of his age.

[Brownstone.]
Here lies Buried the Body of
94 —Sam'l. Hanford Esqr
who died Febr. ye 2nd. 1751 in
ye 77th year of his Age.

[Samuel Hanford was born April 5,
1674 and d. Feb 2d 1751. Married
Isabel "Haynes," "Haines," or
"Hanes," &c. He was a Capt. of Mili-
tia, Justice of the Peace, &c.
His children mentioned in his will,
were :
I. Samuel, b. 1710, d. Mar 28, 1795.
II. Thadeus.
III. Haynes.
IV. Hezekiah, b. 1722 d. May 2, 1812. Aged 90.
[See his wife No 83.]
V. William
VI. Isabel Married Jonathan Hall of New
Haven, died 1749.]

[There no No 95]

[Slate.]
Here Lyes Buried the Body of
96 —Mr. William Hanes
aged 64 years. Died April ye
2d. 1712.

[William Haynes [96] sailed from Lon-
don Jan 8, 1685 on board the Betty,
James May Captain. He made his
will April 1st. 1712 n which he men-
tions his daughter's Elizabeth wife of
John Bartlett, Isabel the wife of
Samuel Hanford [94] and Mary
Haynes who was the daughter of his
last wife who died 1711. The Prop-
erty mentioned in the will was devided Nov 8, 1749. (See his wife No
91).]

[Brownstone.]
Here lies Buried the Body of
97 —Capt. Samuel Comstock
who Departed this life October
the 26th. 1752 in the 73d. year of
his age

[Capt. Samuel Comstock above mentioned was a Son in Law of Rev
Thomas Hanford having married his
youngest daughter Sarah Dec. 27,
1705. She was born May 1677.]

98 —Sadie
Daughter of C. H, Hendrick

99 —[Clarkie Hendrick]
Son of C. H. Hendrick

[Brownstone.]
Here Lies the Body of
100 —Mrs Sarah Darrow
Wife of Mr John Darrow who
died Decembr 11, 1749 in the
34th ye'r of her age

101 —Henrietta. D. Andrews
Born May 7th, 1833, Died Jan.
16th, 1886.

[Small Marble Monument.]
101½ —Our Little Harry
Died Oct. 2, 1878, Æ. 6 yrs. 5
mos, & 10 Days,
The Lord gaveth and hath taken.

102 —Willie [Hendrick]
Son of C. H. Hendrick

103 —Maria Davids
Born Aug. 21st, 1805, Died June
8th, 1885.

[Slate.]
HERE Lyes ye Body of
104 —Mary Marven
Wife of John Marven aged 35
years. Departed This life April
ye 17th, 1720.

In memory of
105 —Sidney S. Kugler
Died Aug. 14, 1877, aged 20 ys,
10 m's and 3 D's.

[Brownstone.]
106 —Mrs Mary St John
the wife of — Mr James St John
Dec'd Oct'r 17th. 1749 in ye 76
year of her age.

[Brownstone.]
In memory of
107 —Polly [Eversley]
Daughter of John & Mary
Eversley who died Sep'r 3d. 1801
aged 1 year & 8 mo.

In memory of
108—*Daniel Eversley*
who died Sept. 23, 1825. Æ. 85
years.

[Brownstone.]
Here lies the Body of
109—*Mrs Mercy Saint John*
Wife of Mr Moses Saint John
who died Nov'r ye 23d. 1748.
aged 37 years & 8 months

110—*Hannah. M. [Weed]*
Wife of Harvey S. Weed Died.
April 1, 1887, Æ, 62 yrs. 6 mos.
& 23 Ds.

Dear Mother at Rest

[Brownstone.]
In memory of
111—*John Eversley*
who died May 17th, 1798 in the
62d. year of his age.

In memory of
112—*Abigail Eversley,*
who died Oct. 9, 1821. Æ T.
84 years.
—:o:—

In memory of
113—*John Eversley,*
who died Feb. 22, 1836, in the
70, year of his age.

114—*Harriet A. [Camp]*
Wife of Rev Harvey Camp, Died
July 31, 1886.

[Stone fallen on ground.]
115—*John Eversley*
Died Aug. 26. 1848, Æ. 51 y's,
& 5 Ds.
—:o:—

[Brownstone.]
Here lies the Body of
116—*Mrs Deborah [Mead]*
the wife of Leut'n Nehemiah
Mead who died July ye 3d. 1749
in ye 40th. year of her age

117—*Willis D. [Gregory]*
Son of George W. and Eliza J.
Gregory, Died Aug. 19, 1864,
Æ, 1 y'r 8 mo's. & 20 Days.

[Other side of stone]
Our Willie
Grand son of Rev. Z. & E.
Davenport.

[Stone Broken on the ground.]
In memory of
118—*Mary [Eversley]*
wife of John Eversley, who died
Aug. 21, 1857, in the 88th, year
of her age.

119—*John B. Gregory*
Died July 22, 1842, Æ. 59 y'rs,

[Little monument.]
120—*R. Edwin [Carman]*
Son of Samuel & Irene Carman,
Born May 13, 1884, Died Oct.
7, 1884,
Our Baby.

[Small marble monument.]
Our Darling.
121—*Zophar S. [Carman]*
Son of Samuel & Irene Car-
man Born Feb. 24, 1878, Died
Dec. 10, 1884.

122—*Mary. J. A. [Hoyt.]*
Wife of William B. Hoyt Died
Feb 5, 1889.
"Precious Jesus"

123—*Bertha May [Evenden]*
Daughter of James & Elizabeth
Evenden. Born Dec. 18, 1882.
Died Feb. 17, 1891.

124—*George. F.*

125—*Mother*

126—*Olive*
Wife of John B. Gregory, Born
Oct. 18, 1785, Died Feb. 1, 1881.

127—*Bertha A. [Hine]*
daughter of U. W. & E. L. Hine
Died Jan. 9, 1888. Æ. 2 yrs.
& 7, mo's.

[Other side of stone.]
Darling Bertha
Safe in the arms of Jesus
Sister.

128—*Jane Stuckey*
Died August 15, 1881. Aged 28 years 10 months, and 15 days.

[There is no No 129.]

130—*Charles F. G. Gregory*,
Died March 5, 1845, aged 25 y'rs.

Nancy.
Wife of Charles F. G. Gregory, Died March 22, 1890, aged 75 y'rs.

131—*Charles. F. Gilbert*
Died Aug: 10, 1881, Æ. 30 y'rs, 8 mo's. and 26 Days.

Lord remember me when thou comest into thy Kingdom

[Slate.]
Here lie ye Remains of
132—*Mr. Seth Smith*.
Who departed this Life May the 7th 1772. aged 31 years.

[Quincy Granite.]
133—*John G. Cooper*,
Born Sept. 19, 1828, Died Oct. 13, 1860.

Margaret E.
His wife Born July 23, 1833, Died June 2, 1891.

Mary Emily
Their infant daughter, aged 7 weeks.

In after-time we'll meet them.
COOPER

In memory of
134—*Eliza S.*
Daughter of Capt. Samuel., and Elizabeth. S. Page. who died Sept, 13, 1842. Æ. 7 years 6 mos. and 10 Days.

A widowed mother's lovely child
Last of my earthly Ties,
I placed her in certain hope
To meet her in the Skies.

135—*Samuel Page*
died May 12, 1835, Æ 2 years 8 mo. and 12 days. Son of Capt. Samuel and Sarah. E. Page

In memory of
136—*Charles L, White 2d*
who died Jan, 15, 1834, aged 25 ye, 7 mo. and 20 d's.

In memory of
137—*Mary L, [White]*
daughter of Charles L. & Sally White who died April 4, 1835, Æ. 6 mos. & 4 ds

In memory of
138—*Harriet H. [Kelly]*
Daughter of William & Esther Kelly who Died July 21, 1839. Æ 18 years

In memory of
138½—*Sally (Mallory) [White]*
Widow of Charles L, White. & daughter of John & Hannah, J Mallory who died July 31, 1855. aged 43 years 9 mo, & 17 days.

In memory of
139—*Samuel [Mallory]*
Son of John & Hannah Mallory who died June 1, 1810 Æ. 1 mo. and 21 ds.

In memory of
140—*Mary Mallory*
who died Nov. 10, 1795. Æ. 45 years
wife of Matthew Mallory who was lost at sea 1781.

141—*Charles [Mallory]*
Son of Lewis & Anna Mallory died Jan. 31, 1800, Æ. 6 years & 2 mo.

In memory of
142—*Lewis Mallory*,
who died July 21, 1838, aged 69 years 10 months & 10 days.

143—*Harriet (Hulin) [Mallory]*
wife of Rev. George. H. Hulin and daughter of Lewis and Anna Mallory died April 1, 1836, Æ. 25 years.

Doubting Christian cast thyself upon the devine assurance "My grace is sufficient for thee" then, as did she in thy dying day thou shalt have dying grace.

143½—*Florence. N,* [*Raymond*]
Dau of Edward and Georgianna
Raymond. — Died — Jan. 9,
1888, Æ. 8 yrs, 4 mo. & 13
days

Safe in the arms of Jesus.

144—*Polly Thorp* [*Mallory*]
Daughter of Matthew and Mary
Mallory Died August 4, 1868.
Æ. 93 y'rs. and 10 m's.

In memory of
145—*Anna Mallory*
wife of Lewis Mallory, who
died Jan. 3, 1848, Æ. 75 y'rs,
11 mo's. and 22 Days,

146—*George Lewis* [*Hulin*]
Son of Rev. George H. & Harriet Hulin died Nov. 14, 1835.
Æ. 4 months & 3 days.

In memory of
147—*Hannah Jarvis,* [*Mallory*]
wife of John Mallory, who died
Sept. 7, 1851. Æ. 65 years 6
mo. & 2 Days

To the memory of
148—*Daniel* [*Mallory*]
son of John and Hannah Mallory who died July 7, 1838. Æ.
21 years 10 mos & 9 Days.

In memory of
149—*John Mallory,*
who died March 23, 1846, Æ.
66 years 9 mo. & 23 Days.

150—*William Mallory*
Died July 31, 1859, aged 51
years & 7 months.

Farewell, farewell, to the a long and last adieu
In deaths dark hour, where earthly scenes are
    fadeing from my view
Thy blessed spirit, hovering near, shall soar
    with mine above,
Where fadeless flowers forever bloom, and all
    is peace and love.

[Quincy Granite.]
151—*Sarah Husted*
wife of Capt. A. B. St John Died
Sept, 23rd 1886.

"Dearest sister thou hast left us.
And thy loss we deeply feel,
But 'tis God that hast bereft us
He will all our sorrows heal."

In memory of
152—*Amelia E. Smith*
Daughter of John L. & Jane
Smith, who died Feb. 7, 1839.
In the 21. year of her age.

Jesus can make a dying bed,
Feel soft as downy pillows are,
While on his breast I lean my head
And breath my life out sweetly there

153—*Jane*
wife of John L. Smith Died
Sept. 3d, 1887, Æ. 93 years.

154—*John. L. Smith*
Died Dec. 7, 1872. aged 86
years 1 mo. & 2 Days,

Blessed are the dead who die in the Lord

155—*Luther. M Lockwood*
son of Sylvester B. & Emily
F. Lockwood Æ. 6 months &
20 days

Not lost but gone before.

156—*Thomas Cornwall*
Died Dec. 12, 1815, Æ 75
— :0 :—
So teach us to number our days that we
may apply our hearts unto wisdom.

In memory of
157—*Mary B. Cornwall*
who died Feb. 20, 1826, in the
20 year of her age.

The hope of her eternal bless
edness gives comfort and supp
ort, to an afflicted and discon
solate mother.

In memory of
158—*Josiah Cornwall*
who died Feb 8, 1820 Æ 34

159—*Francis B.* [*St John*]
Son of Oscar and Mary D. St
John. Died Sept. 23, 1870, Æ.
1 y'r 9 mo's and 25 Days.

[Other side.]
Little Frank

160—*Charles Cook St John*
Died Mar. 17, 1876. Æ. 61
years 11 mo's and 3 Days,
"Servant of God well done"

In memory of

161—Elizabeth [McNiel]

daughter of Robert. A. & Sarah Ann McNiel, who died July 1, 1845, Æ. 16 years 5 mo, & 26 Days,

Peace 'tis the Lord Jehovah's hand
That blasts our joys in death,
That mars that form to us so dear
And gathers back the dust.

162—Sarah A. [Rockwell] [McNiel]

Widow of Eli Rockwell, and formerly wife of Robert A. McNiel. Died Aug. 23, 1886, Æ. 57 years 2 mo's & 10 Days.

163—Mary E. [Richards] [McNiel]

wife of Joseph S. Richards, & daughter of Robert A, & Sarah Ann McNiel Died May 25, 1866, aged 32 years.

"In life beloved, in death lamented."

Edward Townsend [Richards]

only son of Joseph S, & Mary E. Richards, Died May 16, 1870, Æ. 4 y'rs & 7 m's.

164—Robert A. McNiel,

Died Feb. 3, 1837 in the 30th year of his age.

Mary McNiel,

died May 10, 1831, Æ. 2 years and 2 mo.

David McNiel,

Died Dec. 18, 1836, Æ. 7 mo. Children of Robert A. and Sarah Ann McNiel.

[Slate.]

165—Mr. Samuel Hayes

aged 72 years Dec'd April ye 7 1712.

[Slate.]

Here lyes the Remains of

166—John Copp Esqr,

Deacon of ye first church in this place, who Departed this Life May ye 16th Anno Domni 1751. in ye 78th year of his age.

When the archangel shall aloud proclaim,
The total ruin of the worlds great Frame,
And gastly Horrours seize this trembling ball,
And frighted stars shall from their centers fall
Then the last Trump shall raise the conscious Dead
And thou hold man shalt hide thy guilty head
Such humble saints shall wake with glad surprise
To meet their Saviour from the bending skies.

[Marble monument.]

167—Martha, A Saxon

wife of William E. Root Died July 11, 1876, Æ. 52 y'rs. & 10 mo's.

Root

Matthew Saxon
Died June 22, 1882. Æ. 58 y'rs & 9 mo's.

Saxon

Isaac T.
Died Aug 30, 1861. Æ. 12 y'rs & 1 mo's.

Mathew S.
Died Oct. 20, 1862. Æ. 11 yrs. & 7 mo's
Children of Wm. E & Martha A. Root

[Brownstone.]

Here lies Buried the Body of

168—Joseph Platt Esqr

who Departed this life 12th June 1748 in the 76 year of his age.

[Slate.

168½—Easter Lines

Dau to Benja'h & Easer Lines aged 2 Years 11 Mo & 12 Das Decd. May ye 22d 1722

[Granite monument.]

169—Charles. J, Saunders

Born May 15, 1791 Died June 6, 1874.

Orindia Saunders

Born Oct. 10, 1810 Died Nov. 25, 1884

170—Martha H. (Disbrow) [Platt])

Wife of Henry G. Disbrow and Daughter of Alfred & Abigail Platt. Died June 8, 1882, In the 24 year of her age
Safe in the arms of Jesus

171--Bertha [Platt]
Daughter of Alfred & Abigail
Platt. Died May 7. 1877, Æ.
2 years, 7 mo's. & 10 Days.

Little Birdie,
Beautiful Birdie,
lamb of the blest,
Jesus has taken thy
pure spirit to rest.

172--Reuben L. [Platt]
Son of Alfred and Abigail Platt.
Born Jan, 18, 1853, Died Nov.
25, 1872,

Our loved one.

173- Jacob Reynolds
Died July 17, 1885, aged 74 yrs.
& 8 mo's.

—:o:—

174--Lucinda [Reynolds]
Wife of Jacob Reynolds Died
Jan. 9, 1882, aged 69 yrs. 2. mo's.
& 8 Ds.

In memory of
175--Rebecca E. [McLean]
Daughter of Hugh & Angeline
McLean who died July 21,
1827. Æ. 1 year & 7 mo
An empty tale a morning flow'r,
Cut down and wither'd in an hour.

176--Sarah A. Fitch
Wife of William E. Fitch. Born
March 5, 1848, Died February 3,
1875.

177--Samuel M. Fitch.
Died Feb. 12, 1857, Æ. 87 y'rs.

178--Betsey Fitch, [Roberts]
Wife of David Roberts, Died
May 2, 1869, aged 65 years.
—:o:—

179--Mary. A, Quin
Died D'ec 25, 1884 Aged 23 y'rs.
& 9 mo's,

180--J, A, Ames
Co. D 7th Conn. Inf.

181--Emily. [Fitch]
daughter of Samuel M. Jr. &
Mary Fitch, Died Sept. 27, 1836.
Æ. 2 y'rs.

182—Samuel, M. Fitch Jr
Died May 18, 1854, Æ. 54 yrs,

183—Esther [Fitch]
wife of Samuel M. Fitch, Died
June 3, 1854, Æ. 74 y'rs.

184—Rebecca E, [Fitch]
Daughter of Daniel & Sarah
Fitch. Died April 13, 1882, Æ
48 y'rs 8 mo's.
Safe in the arms of Jesus.

185—Sarah Fitch
wife of Daniel Fitch, Died Dec.
1869, aged 60 years and 3 m's.
He giveth his beloveth sleep.

186 -Daniel Fitch,
Died July 27, 1885, aged 86 y'rs.
3 mo's. and 25 D's.
He is not dead but sleepeth.

187—Catherine A. [Fitch]
Daughter of Daniel & Sarah
Fitch. Died Feb. 6, 1839, Æ. 3
y'rs and 5 D's.
Then rest the loved one, rest
Thy warfare soon was o'er
We'll strive thee with the blest
Where sorrows come no more

In memory of
188--Sarah. A, [Fitch]
daughter of Daniel & Sarah
Fitch who died Aug 27, 1826,
Æ 9 mo & 14 days
An empty tale a morning flower
Cut down and withered in an hour

189—Henry Fitch
Died Nov. 10, 1868, Æ. 95 y'rs
9 mo. & 12 D's.

In memory of
190--Ruth Whitney,
Widow of Ebenezer Whitney.
of Revolutionary memory Deceased who departed this life
May 31, 1839, Æ 82 years 6
mo, & 16 Days.

In life of a meek and quiet spirit
in death serene,
Asleep in Jesus O for me
may such a blissful refuge be
securely shall my ashes lie
Waiting the summons from on high

191- Eben Whitney

Born Nov. 19, 1783, Died May 22, 1899,

The law of truth was in his mouth and iniquity was not found on his lips he walked with me in peace and equity and did turn many away from iniquity.

In memory of

192 —Emeline [Whitney]

wife of Eben Whitney who departed this life Jan. 9, 1854, Æ. 48 yrs & 7 mos.

193—Abby Fitch

wife of Henry Fitch. Died Dec. 22, 1858, Æ. 63 y'rs 6 mo & 14 D's.

[Slate broken.]

In memory of

194 Jonothan Fitch A. M

who departed this life July 7th AD 1773 in the 30th year. of his age youngest son of Samuel Fitch Esqr.

195—Edwin W. Fitch,

Son of Daniel & Sarah Fitch, Died Aug. 2, 1870, Æ. 38 y'rs & 10 mo's.

Blessed are those servants whom the lord when he cometh shall find watching.

[Granite headstone]

196 —Theodore Wilcox

died June 17, 1882, aged 45 yrs. 9 mo. & 19 Days

"Be thou faithful unto Death"

197—Frances J. [Fitch]

wife of George W. Fitch. Died June 21st 1888, Æ. 44 years 5 mo's.

"The Lord gave, and the Lord hath taken away, blessed be the name of the LorL"

Mother.

198—Elizabeth I. Van Name

Died Jan. 10, 1890, Æ. 62 years.

[Quincy Granite monument.]

199—Lewis Raymond

Born July 21, 1807, Died Nov. 20, 1881.

His wife

Catherine Merker

Born Dec. 9, 1811, Died Nov. 18. 1871.

Raymond

Platt Raymond Born Dec. 3, 1774, Died Dec. 6, 1857.

His wife

Hannah S. Benedict

Born Jan. 4, 1779, Died April 27, 1844.

Their Children

Jesse B. Raymond

Born April 17, 1799, Died Aug. 8, 1872.

Alfred Raymond

Born Jan. 27, 1802, Died Oct. 20, 1828,

Mehetable Raymond

Born Oct. 25. 1804. Died March 29, 1888

Children of Lewis & Catherine M, Raymond

Hannah M, Raymond

Born Nov. 9, 1835, Died June 29, 1843.

Charles, Raymond

Born Dec. 21, 1837, Died. Jan. 5, 1869.

200 - William R. Knapp

Co. C. 5, Regt. Conn. Vols. Died Dec 28, 1891.

201—Josephine [Knapp]

Daughter of Charles & Huldah Knapp. Died Aug. 5, 1857, age 10 Days.

202—Charles Knapp

Died Aug. 24. 1860, Æ. 42 yrs & 3 mo's.

When trials do surround you, And troubles cross your way, Then cast your cares on Jesus, And dont forget to pray.

203—Charles, E. Knapp,
a member of Company D, 13th
Reg., Conn. Vol. Died March
18, 1862, Æ. 19 yrs. 5 mo's. and
7 D'ys.

Sleep Soldier still in honored rest .
Your truth and valor wearing :
The bravest are the tenderest
The loveing are the dareing.

204—J. E. Lacey
Co. C 25th Conn. Inf.

205—Nathaniel Fisher
Died Oct. 18, 1888, Æ. 58 years
& 2 mo's

Our father at rest.

Sister.

206—Anna Warren
Sept. 29, 1847. Oct. 11, 1891.

She sought not her own comfort ;
but that of others.

In memory of
207—Wm Francis [Hull]
Son of Isaac P. & Henrietta
Hull who Died Sept. 4, 1846,
aged 7, years and 10 Days.

[Brownstone.]

Here Lyeth the Body of the Rever

**207½—Mr Jedeiah Bucking-
ham**
Late preachr' of The Gospel at
the West Part of New ark in
East Jersey Who Depar'ed This
Life March the 28th 1720
Æ TATIS SU—24

[Quincy Granite monument.]
Hooker

208—Mary Willett [Hooker]
Daughter of Capt. Thomas
Willett Who was the first mayor
of the City of New York Wife
of Rev. Samuel Hooker of
Farmington Conn From her
sons came all Hookers who are
descended From Rev. Thomas
Hooker First settler of Hartford
Conn. Born at Plymouth Mass.
November 10th 1637 Married
at Plymouth Mass. Sep 22ND
1658 Died at Norwalk Conn
June 24th 1712
This stone is erected by her
descendents 1890

[Other side is inscribed.]
Near here are buried
**Rev. Stephen Bucking-
ham**
and his wife Sarah Hooker.
Daughter of Rev, Samuel and
Mary W. Hooker also
Josiah Hooker
and his wife Hannah he a
great-grand son of Rev. Samuel
and Mary W. Hooker.

[Slate broken—Supplied with an Iron
Back.]

Here lyes buried the Body of the
Rev'd
**209—Mr Stephe[n] Bucking-
ham**
late Pastor of the 1st Church of
Christ in Norwalk departed
this life F—bry 3d 1745-6
Æ tatis 70.

[Brownstone.]
Here lies the Body of
210—Mr Thomas Hanford
ye Eldest son of ye Revd Mr
Thomas Hanford who died June
ye 7 A D 1743 in ye 75 year of his
his age with Hannah his wife
lving at his rite hand who
Dec'd Dec'r 28 1745 aged 78 years
& 5 days

[The Rev Thomas Hanford was the 1st
Pastor of the first church in Norwalk
and was ordained 1652. (Cotton
Mather says—he was Educated in
England). His mother Eglin Hanford aged 46 a widow come to Amer-
ica in 1635. "She embarked at Lon-
don 10 April 1635 on the Planter,
Nicholas Trarice Master. She
brought with her, two daughters
Margaret aged 16 and Elizabeth aged
14. She afterwards married Deacon
Richard Sealis of Situate, Mass," her
son Thomas is known to have been
in Mass in 1643—and taught school
there. "Thomas Hanford married
1st Hannah dau of Thomas Newbury
of Dorchester, no issue is heard of
by her ; 2nd married Oct 22—1661
Mary widow of Jonathan Ince the
New Haven scholar." She d. 1723 or
before. He died probably before
1693, and is said to have been buried
under a brownstone tablet lying
close to the ground near where his
son Thomas was buried [210].
His children were :
I. Theophilus b. July 29—1662 "went to
parts unknown [Probate Reeds].
II. Mary b. Nov 30—1663 married John Ed-
wards of Fairfield.
III. Hannah b. June 28, 1665.

[Slate.]
Here lyes Buried the Body of
211—Capt. Elnathan Hanford
who departed this life August
ye 24th 1764 in ye 58th year of
his age.

[Brownstone.]
212—Mary [Hanford]
the Daughter of Elna & Sarah
Hanford Dec'd Novr ye 27,
1750 in ye 3rd year of her age
Oh now sweet Babe
Because twas best
God took you home
With him to Rest

[Slate.]
213—Elizabeth Thatcher
Daughtr of Mr Josiah & Mrs
Mary Thatcher Died Septembr
5 1743 aged 6 years 4 months &
10 Days

In memory of
214—Henrietta, [Hull (Gibbs)]
wife of Isaac P, Hull &
daughter of Horace A. & Julia
Ann Gibbs who died April 24.
1842 Æ. 26 years 7 mo & 26
Days,
Therefor be ye also ready for in such
an hour as ye think not Son of man
cometh.—Mat 24, 44.

In memory of
215—Julia Ann Gibbs,
wife of Horace A. Gibbs, who
died Feb. 4, 1833, Æ. 38 years.

In memory of
216—Stephen St John
who died Aug, 27, 1828, Æ 66
years.

In memory of
217—Sally, [St John]
wife of Stephen St John. who
died Oct. 22. 1825. Æ, 59
years.

[Double Brownstone.]
In memory of
218—Thomas Fitch Esqr
who died Janry 16th 1795 [or 93]
in the 70th year of his age

In memory of
Sarah
wife of Thomas Fitch Esqr who
died Janry 27th 1795 in the 61st
year of her age

[Granite]
Mabel
219—Mabel. G. [Mead]
Daughter of George E. & Ella G,
Mead, Oct. 21, 1882, Sept. 29,
1891.

Alas the fairest fade early.

[Slate.]
Here Lyes Buried the body of
220—Mrs Ann Thatcher
wife to Mr. Josiah Thatcher
aged 34 years & 11 MO, Deed
Febry ye 25 1733-4

[Slate.]
In memory of
221—Mrs Mary Thacher,
wife of Cap, Josiah Thacher,
who departed this Life April 6th
AD 1774, in her 68th year.
Who follow here, ye paths of trnth,
Shall Bloom in everlasting youth,
Clad with new Glories they shall shine,
In charms immortal and devine.

[Slate.]
Here lyes Buried the Body of
222—John Betts Esqr,
who departed this Life June the
7th 1745 aged 60 years & 11
months,

[Brownstone.]
222½—Mrs. Hannah Betts.

[Brownstone]
223—Thaddeus Hill Fitch
son of Tha's & Sarah Fitch died
Oct 21—1776 age 11 months

[Brownstone]
224—Hannah [Fitch]
Daughter of Mr Thomas & Mrs
Hannah Fitch who Departed
this life on the 24th of August
1744 in the [14 or 17] year of her
age is here buried

[Slate.]

225—*Giles Fitch*

son of Mr Thomas & Mrs Hannah Fitch who departed this life in April 1747 in ye 2nd year of his age and in here interred

[Slate.]

Here lyes Interred the Body of

226—*Ebenezer Fitch*

who departed this life Febry 23d AD 1762 in ye 33d year of his age

[Slate.]

Here lyes interred the body of

227—*Mrs Hannah Fitch*

who departed this life August ye 7th 1769 in ye 25th year of Her age.

Sic Transit Gloria Mundi

[Slate.]

228—*Miss Esther Fitch*

Daghter of the HonBle Thomas Fitch and Hannah Fitch Departed this life on ye 12th of March 1771 in ye 30th year of here age and is here interred

Blessed are ye dead that die in ye Lord

[Brownstone.]

Here lies what was mortal of

229—*Mrs Martha Paddock*

wife of Mr. Enoch Paddock & Daugt of ye Revd Mr Moses Dickenson who died July 15 1752 in ye 18 year of her age

[A Tomb Table of Brownstone on 5 pillars and Slate inserted in the Table.]

230—*THE HON'BLE THOMAS Fitch Esqr*

Gov'r of the Colony of CONNECTICUT Eminent, and distinguished among mortals, For great abilities, large aquirements and a virtuous character; a clear, strong, sedate mind; an accurate, extensive acquaintance with Law and civil Government; a happy Talent of presiding; close application, and strict fidelity in the the discharge of important Trusts; no less than, for his employments, by the voice of the people, in the chief offices of State, and at the HEAD of the COLONY. Having served his generation by the Will of God fell asleep July 18th, AnD Domini, 1774. in the 75th Year of his age.

[Governor Thos Fitch was son of Thomas. He married Sep 4, 1724. Hannah Hall of New Haven the eldest dau of Richard and Hannah (Miles) Hall). The Hou'ble Thomas was the Governor's assistant 1734-5 and from 1740 to 1754 when he was elected Governor, May, the same year and remained as such to May 1765 when he came back to Norwalk lived, and probably died, at what is now known as the old Fitch place, on East ave. a little south of opposite the East entrance to the road leading to Oyster Shell point. A large elm tree is seen in front of the house as a landmark undisturbed to his memory.

231—*Halsey Day*

Died Dec. 17th, 1883, Æ. 32 years 6 mo's. & 4 Days.

Papa

[Slate.]

RELIQUIÆ

232—*Moses Dickenson*

HIC Deponuntur OBIIT sep 16 1742 ÆTAT 20

[Slate.]

Here lyes what was mortal of

233—*Mrs Martha Dickenson*

wife to ye Revnd Mr. Moses Dickenson Who Died Decembr 15th Anno Domi 1755 Ætates 62

[Brownstone.]

Beneath this monumental stone lies interred the body of the

234—*Revd. Moses Dickenson,*

late pastor of the first Church of Christ in NORWALK, who departed this life May 1st. 1778. in the 83d. year of his age, and 51st fo his Ministry in said church.

A man of a good Understanding, well improved by Study, Chearfull in Temper Prudent in Conduct and faithfull to his trust He came to his grave in full age, like as a shock of corn cometh in his season.

In memory of

234½—*Eliza F. Christian*

who departed this life November 26th. 1809 Aged 20 Years 7 months & 22 days

In memory of

235—*Timothy Fitch*

who died Sept 18, 1802 in the 67 year of his age

+

236—Esther [Fitch]
Relict of Timothy Fitch died
May 5, 1816. Æ 71.

In memory of
237—Cornelia, [Fitch]
wife of Stephen Fitch, who Died
Sept. 12. 1811, Æ. 49 yrs.

238—Edward Fitch
Died July 23, 1808. Æ. 36 y's.
Mary E. his wife Died Jan. 9,
1841, Æ. 67 y's.
This stone is erected by their child An-
jinette Hall of Troy, N. Y.

239—Hannah [Belden]
Wife of Azar Belden, died
March 29, 1860, Æ. 93 y'rs 6
mo's & 14 D's.

[Granite monument.]
240—Mr Samuel Marvin
Died Nov. 8, 1820, Æt. 80.
—:o:—

241—Susannah Fitch
Died May 24, 1888, Æ. 83 yrs,
1 mo, & 11 Ds,

James Fitch
Died July 31, 1828, Æ. 70 yrs, 3
mos & 20 ds.

Esther Camp
His wife Diep Sept. 9. 1846
Æ. 83 yrs, 6 mos, & 17 Ds.

Julia Fitch
Died June 23, 1857 Æ, 57 yrs. 4
mos. & 13 Ds.

[Granite monument.]
242—Col. Henry Rogers
Died Apr. 27, 1857, aged 71.

243—William Francis [Das-kam]
son of Capt, Samuel & Lucretia
Daskam, Died Oct. 13, 1856. Æ. 38.
He has gone to the grave as tenderly loved
As any that ever from earth was removed
And when the last call to us shall be given
Oh may we be ready to meet him in Heaven.

244—Capt, Samuel Daskam.
Died April 21, 1858, aged 71
years 6 mo. & 11 Days.

245—Theodolia [Fitch]
daughr of Josiah II, & Ann P.
Fitch, died April 30, 1816 Æ 17.
The firmest rock is now on high
And for all nature he did die
The fairest Plant the fairest flower
Cut down and wither'd in an hour.
—:o:—

246—Josiah H. Fitch
Died Dec. 1, 1845, Æ. 76.

ANN PLATT, wife of Josiah H.
Fitch, died oct. 20, 1845. Æ. 73.

"They were lovely and pleasant in their lives
and in their death they were not devided,"

In memory of
247—Mary [Conklin]
wife of Jonas P, Conklin. who
died Aug. 19, 1832: Æ. 24 years.

In memory of
248—Samuel Hanford
who died Aug 7, 1833. Æ. 58.

249—Sarah [Hanford]
wife of Samuel Hanford died
April 14, 1823: aged 51 years.

In memory of
250—Hezekiah Hanford
who died Jan 16, 1811: Æ 57.
—:o:—

[Stone Broken]
In memory of
251—Sarah [Hanford]
wife of Hezk Hanford who died
Dec. 25, 1811 Æ 59

252—Elnathan Hanford

died Nov. 19, 1800, Æ 24.
—:o:—
[He was son of Hezekiah.]

253—David Hanford

died Dec. 15, 1815, Æ 27

—:o:—

254—Polly [Hoyt (Hanford)]
wife of Ira Hoyt. & widow of
David Hanford, died Aug. 25,
1820. Æ. 40 years.

255—Sarah [(Nash) Van Hoo-
sear]

wife of David V Hoosen

[David Van Hoosear]
and widow of Elnathan Hanford [See 252] Died May 14,
1817: in her 30th year.

She was dau of Daniel and Freelove
(Wright) Nash—whose residence was
Norwalk—(now Westport, Ct.) She
died at "Grumman Hill" Wilton,
Conn. As wife of Elnathan she had
3 children—Dennis—Mary—and Sal-
ly. Her only child, as wife of David
Van Hoosear, was David Nash Van
Hoosear born May 1st, 1817. Alive
1893. Res. Wilton, Ct.

256—Elizabeth [Hanford]

wife of Charles Hanford, died
Feb. 20, 1831, Æ. 18 years.

257—William H. Hanford

born Feb. 7, 1840, died Nov. 1,
1866.

The Lord gave and the Lord hath taken away.

258—Mary Priscilla [Godfry]

Daughter of Silliman & Priscilla B. Godfrey Died March 24,
1875 Æ. 21 y'rs, 6 mo's & 7 days.

She sleepeth ! so silently !
In the last and peacefull rest,
Her sun has set, while yet 'twas day,
Her gentle spirit has soared away
For the angels loved her best.

259—Thomas Fitch

Son of Edward & Sarah Fitch &
Grandson of Samuel M. & Es-
ther Fitch Born Mar 13 1843
Died May 30, 1888.

Served his country During the war as
Capt. Co. H. 93rd N. Y. V. 3d Brigade
3d Division, 3d Army Corps.

260—Francis Jones,

Died March 24, 1865, aged 32
y'rs 3 mo's & 17 Days.

He served in Co. G, 28 Reg. Conn. Vols.

261—Little Willie.

Died June 27, 1872, aged 7
months.

[Double stone]

262—Frank [Howland]

born Jan. 3, 1856, died Aug. 21,
1858.

Ella A.

born June 11, 1868, died Feb 16,
1872.

Children of J. H. & Nancy. J.
Howland

"Suffer littly children to come unto me,"

263—Ida J,

Daughter of Cornelius & Elizabeth J, Van Name Died Aug.
3, 1872, Æ. 15 years 2 mo's & 23
Days.

At R st.

[Marble monument.]

Erected 1880

264—T. Raymond

Edith

265—Edith May [Raymond]

Daughter of F. M. & E. R.
Raymond Died July 31, 1890,
Æ. 7 Mo's & 9 Days.

266—Eunice [Bradley]

daughter of Clark & Mary Brad-
ley, died Aug. 20, 1866, Æ. 17
y'rs 1 mo. & 10 D's.

Jesus to thy dear faithfull hand,
My naked soul I trust :
My flesh shall wait for thy command
And drop into my dust.

267—Grace. M. [Smith]

Daughter of Charles W. & Emily,
H. Smith Died Jan. 28, 1882,
Æ. 5 yrs, 10 mos, & 16 Days

Little Gracie was our darling,
Pride of all the hearts at home,
But the Angels whispered softly
Gracie come.
Little Gracie

[Brownstone.]

Here lies the Remains of

268—Capt, John Raymond

who was Born Seper ye 18th 1664
and Put on immortality April ye
12th 1737

[Slate.]

Here lyes ye Body of

269—Mrs Mary Street

Relict to Mr Nathaniel Street
who departed this Life March
7th 1762 in ye 67th year of Her
age

[Slate.]
Here Lyes Buried ye Body of
270—Mr Nathan'el Street
who Departed this life Sep 24,
1748 in ye 56th year of his age

[Brownstone.]
271—Elizabeth [Street]
ye Daughter of Mr. Nathaniel &
Mrs Mary Street Dec'd March
19—1738 aged 19 yrs

272—Edith May [Beers]
daughter of Wm. P. & Cornelia
A. Beers Died Dec. 9, 1875.
Æ. 5 yrs 1 mo, & 19 Days
Safe in the arms of Jesus

273—Our Little Robbie [Jones]

274—Alice [Jones]

275—Edgar [Jones]

276—Fletcher [Jones]
[The above 4 are children of
Henry Jones of East Norwalk,
Conn.]

In memory of
277—Mary. F, [Hoyt]
wife of James Winship, &
daughter of Francis & Nancy
Hoyt, who died Nov, 13, 1846.
Æ. 24 y'rs

In memory of
278—Rosanna B,]Hoyt]
Daughter of Francis & Nancy
Hoyt who Died July 25, 1851,
Æ. 17 y'rs & 9 mo.

279—Amanda. L. Hoyt
wife of Titus K, Merrill, Died
May 1, 1881, Æ, 57 y'rs, 2 mos &
20 Days
At Rest.

280—Titus K, Merrill
Died March 27, 1890. Æ. 84 y'rs,
6 mo's. & 15 Days
Blessed are the dead who die in the Lord

281—Francis Hoyt
Died June 17, 1842 Æ 44 y'rs
4 mo's & 14 Days

In memory of
282—Goold [Hoyt]
son of Frances & Nancy Hoyt
who died Oct. 26, 1825, Æ,2 mo,
& 4 days, Also of

William Conklin,
who died April 11, 1828 Æ. 1
mo & 17 days

283—Henry. F. [Hoyt]
Died Sept 25 1832, Æ 1 mo &
3 Days,

Marina, L,
Died July 9, 1836 Æ 6 mo & 10
Days

Harriet A,
Died Sept 15. 1840, Æ. 13 mo.
Children of Francis and Nancy
Hoyt

284—Nancy Hoyt
Widow of Francis Hoyt, Died
Jan. 26, 1866, Æ. 65 y'rs 6 mo's
& 9 Days

285—Bertha Augusta, [Hanford]
Daughter of Charles & Mary
Hanford Died Sept. 8, 1875,
Æ. 11 mo's & 13 D's,
For Jesus I named a sweet child
She was fair as roses half blown
He came to my garden and smiled
And tenderly took back his own

286—Anna M. Jones,
wife of Alex. Jones, Died March
8, 1870, Æ. 24 y'rs 8 mo's. & 5
Days.

Minnie E.
daughter of Alex & Anna M,
Jones Died July 24, 1869, Æ. 10
mo's & 3 days.
At rest in Heaven

287—Henry B, Gorham,
Died Jan. 29, 1862, aged 30 Y'rs
& 23 Days.

Mary E, Gorham.
wife of Henry B. Gorham, Died
Dec. 19, 1882, aged 48 y'rs, & 22
Days.
Sleep on loved ones take thy rest,
God called thee home when he though best,

287½ – *Charles* [*Gorham*]
Son of Henry B, & Mary E,
Gorham. Died Aug. 11, 1864,
aged 6 yrs 3 mo. & 10 Days,

In memory of
288 – *John H. Fitch :*
who died March 26th 1860, aged
65 years 5 mo. & 20 Days.

[Marble monument.]
289 – *Lucretia*,
wife of Hiram C, Jones, Born.
Aug, 7, 1807

Hiram C, Jones,
Born Sept, 10, 1806, Died April
8, 1882
– + –
Jones
Lewis Jones,
Born June 17. 1844, Died Oct.
2, 1891,

A private in Co. E. 5th Conn. Regt.
1861.–1865.

In memory of
290 – *Susannah* [*Fitch*]
widow of John H, Fitch who
died Sept 26, 1881, aged 84 years
& 10 mos.

In memory of
291 – *James Davis*, [*Fitch*]
son of John H, & Susannah
Fitch, who died Aug. 28, 1846.
Æ. 18 years 1 mo. & 9 Days.

In memory of
292 – *Charles Fitch*,
son of John H. & Susannah
Fitch, who Died Sept. 2nd, 1860,
aged 36 years 10 mo. & 4 Days.

293 – *Ella B.* [*Fitch*]
Died Aug. 24th, 1860, aged 8
mo.

Emma B.
Died Sept. 20th 1860, aged 8 mo.
& 27 Days.

Children of George B, & Elizabeth H, Fitch,

He shall gather the lambs with his arm
and carry them in his bosom.

Our Katie.
294 – *Katie P,* [*Trownson*]
Daughter of Edmund & Catherine Trownson Died June 28,
1874, Æ. 5 y'rs 5 mo's, & 19
Days.

[Board]
In memory of
295 – *John H Smith*
Son of John H, & Sarah J.
Smith Died Nov. 1st, 1872, aged
2 yrs – ms.

[Board]
296 – *Willie H.* [*Campbell*]
Son of Augustus and Eunice
Campbell who died July 16th
1872 aged 11 mo's & 25 days

[Board]
297 – *Freddie, A,*]*Campbell*]
Son of Augustus and Eunice
Campbell who died April 24th
1874 aged – mo's & 5 days.

298 – *Augustus Campbell*
Died May 8, 1873. Æ. 32 y'es,
& 5 mo's.

Waiting on the other side
299 – *Cornelius S. Voorhis*
Died Oct. 24, 1876, Æ. 40 y'rs,
8 mr's, & 24 days.

All is well.
300 – *William Sheffield*
Died March 31, 1888, aged 33
years.

Faithfull unto death.
301 – *George A, Raymond*
Born Jan. 6, 1807. Died Sept.
29, 1888.

302 – *Huldah Finch*
wife of George A, Raymond
Died Jan. 22, 1890 Æ. 81 yrs 6
mo's.

303 – *Mary E. Raymond*
Born May 6, 1825 Died Feb.
10, 1884

304 – *Jabez Raymond*
Died Aug. 10, 1857, Æ. 78 y'rs
& 3 mo's.

305—Sally [Raymond]
wife of Jabez Raymond, Died
April 27, 1860, Æ. 76 y'rs. 2
mo's, & 14 D's.

306—Platt F. Raymond,
Died March 15, 1862, Æ. 58 y'rs
& 7 mo.

307—Huldah A. [Raymond]
wife of Platt F. Raymond Born
Jan 30, 1823. Died Dec. 4 1880.

308—H. M. Raymond
Co. G 10th Conn. Inf,
[Buried in the Raymond Vault (the
only one in the yard) in which it is
estimated there are buried 26 more
persons.]

309—Lulu Beatrice [Day]
Infant Daughter of Frank F, &
Annie B. Day. Died Oct. 17,
1882. Æ. 7 mo's.

310—Louie F, [Day]
son of Frank F, & Annie B.
Day Died Oct. 2. 1890. Æ 6 yrs.
8 mo's & 15 D's.

Safe in the arms of Jesus.

311—Nicholas A, Everett
Born Feb. 7, 1812, Died March
6, 1872.

312—Sarah Ann, [Smith]
wife of Andrew Smith Died
Nov. 15, 1884, Æ. 59 y'rs, 5
mo's, & 16 Days

[Slate.]
313—RAYMOND
[Top broken off]

[Slate.]
In memory of
314—Hannah [Raymond]
Daughter of Jabez & Rebecca
Raymond who died Septemr
23d, A. D. 1770 in the 31st year
of her age.

In memory of

315—Mary Kip,
who died Oct. 30. 1805, Æ 65
+

316—Arthur W. [Stabell]
son of Frederick P, & Isabella
Stabell, Died Nov, 22, 1876, Æ.
1 year and 12 D's.

In memory of
317—Mary, [Newkirk]
wife of John Newkirk. who
died Sept. 27, 1817 in the 59
year of her age

Let worms devour my wasting flesh.

In memory of
318—John Newkirk
who died Jan. 14, 1818 in the 67.
year of his age.

Though now this flesh and heart hath fail'd,
And mortal life hath ceas'd;
I shall possess within the veil,
A life of joy and peace.

In memory of
319—Garrit H, Newkirk
who died Feb. 1, 1831, Æ. 43
years.

320—Amelia Newkirk
Relict of Garritt H. Newkirk
Died Nov. 8th 1874, In the 87th
year of her age.

In Memory of
321—Polly [Raymond]
wife of Josiah Raymond, who
died May 19, 1809, Æ. 63 years
& 8 mo.

322—Mr. Josiah Raymond
died, May 25, 1824. in his 87
year
—:o:—

323—Clarinda [Raymond]
daughr. of Thomas & Eunice
Raymond, died Jan. 1, 1825 Æ.
26.
Be ye also ready; for in such an hour
as ye think not the son of man cometh.

*324—Hannah Sophia [Han-
ford]*
wife of Dennis Hanford &
daughter of Thomas & Eunice
Raymond died July 8, 1826,
Æ. 20.
Crush'd as a moth beneath thy hand
We moulder to the dust;
Our feble powers can ne'r withstand
And all beauty's lost.

325—Eunice [Smith]
wife of Hezekiah Smith Born
June 16, 1790, Died Sept. 7,
1873.

326—Julia Helme [Smith]
wife of Hezekiah Smith Jr.
Died Feb 9, 1882. Æ. 49 years
& 4 mo's.

*327 — Emma P. [Staples
(Fitch)]*
wife of Wm. B. Staples &
Daughter of Walter J. & Huldah
A, Fitch Died Sept 3, 1877.
Æ, 24 y'rs, & 5 mo's
Our Loved one.

In memory of
328—Silvester J. [Fitch]
son of Walter J. & Huldah A,
A, Fitch, who Died Aug, 16.
1841. Æ. 1 year & 1 mo.

[Marble Monument.]
329—Noah Mosher
Died July 17, 1872, Æ. 64 y'rs
8 mo's & 26 Days.

Mosher.

J. H. B.
329a—Joseph. H, Brown
Died May 20, 1872, Æ. 38 years
8 mo. & 17 Days.

N. A. M.
329b—Naomie A, [Mosher]
Daughter of Noah & Sarah E.
Mosher, Died Mar, 26, 1856.
Æ. 14 years & 8 Days.

W. H. F,
329c—Walter H. [Fisher]
son of Isaac & Damaris E.
Fisher. Died Feb. 12, 1857,
Æ. 1 year & 1 Mo.

W. H. F.
329d— Willie H. [Fisher]
son of Isaac & Damaris E.
Fisher. Died Aug. 28, 1861,
Æ. 2 Years & 1 Mo.

A. M. M.
329e—Alonzo M. [Mosher]
son of Omen E. & Sarah
Mosher Died Dec. 8, 1865,
Æ. 3 Yrs 2 mo. & 23 D's.

S. M.
329f—Sarah [Mosher]
wife of Omen E. Mosher, Died
Jan. 5, 1867, Æ. 38 Y'rs 10 mo.
& 18 D's.

330—Lewis Wilson
Died Sep. 1, 1885, Æ. 68 yrs. 6
mos, 15 Ds. His wife

Mary A, Eldred
Died Apr. 20, 1868, Æ. 54 yrs.
10 mos, 9 Ds.
At Rest.

In memory of
331—Hannah M. [Ketcham]
wife of Theodorus Ketcham,
who Died March 12, 1881, aged
71 years 1 m'o. & 5 Days.
—:o:—
"Shall we meet beyond the river,
Never to part again,"

In memory of
332—Jemima Eldred
who died Oct. 30, 1878, aged 70
. years
—:o:—
She lived for others
Her memory is precious.

In memory of
333—Mary [Smith]
widow of William Smith who
Died Jan. 17, 1844. Æ 92 years
& 8 mo

334—Henry A. Smith
Died Oct. 27, 1873. Æ 35 years

Emily
335—Emily J. [Smith]
Daughter of Henry A, & Emily
J. Smith. Died Sept, 13, 1886.
Æ. 11 y'rs, 2 mo's. & 24 Days.

[Granite]
Mother
336—Mary E. [Wilmot]
wife of Isaac S, Wilmot Died
Feb. 10, 1889. Age 68.

337—Sarah [Smith]
wife of John Smith Died Oct. 9,
1883. Æ. 90 years

In memory of
338—John Smith
who departed this life Jan 18,
1854. Æ. 78 y'rs & 5 Mo's

Sacred to the memory of
339—Elizabeth [Smith]
wife of John Smith who died
Feb. 24, 1836. aged 54 years.

In Memory of
340—Eliza Snedicar [Smith]
Daughter of Hutton & Phebe
Smith Born Feb. 16, 1807. Who
Died Oct. 18, 1882.

In Memory of
341—Elphonzo, [Snedicor]
The only child of Platt & Eliza
Snedicor, who died March 29.
1842. Æ. 2 years 7 Mo, & 29
Days

Tis hard indeed for me to part
With my fair and gentle child
To me so kindly given.

[Granite monument]
342—Thomas Benedict
Died Sept. 13, 1883, Æ. 86 years

Susan [Benedict]
wife of Thomas Benedict Died
June 16, 1876. Æ. 77 years

Mary & Elizabeth
Children of Thos & Susan Benedict

Betsy Ann
wife of Thomas Benedict Died
Nov. 11, 1879. Æ. 62 years
Benedict

In memory of
343—Ebenezer H. Smith,
who died Feb. 21, 1857. Æ. 76
y'rs & 11 mo's.

Sacred to the memory of
344—Susannah [Smith]
wife of Ebenezer H. Smith who
died Aug, 19, 1828, Æ t. 45
years.

345—Harriet N. [Benedict]
widow of David W, Benedict
Died May 6, 1888, aged 59 years
4 mo, & 16 Days.

"Waiting on the other shore."

346—David W Benedict
Died Dec. 28, 1852, aged 24
years 11 mo, & 25 Days.

Sacred to the memory of
347—Ann Eliza, [Bergen]
wife of James Bergen, who died
June 22 1839, aged 22 years.

*348—Francis A, Ralston M.
D.*
Died December 12, 1879, Æ 34
years.

349—Nellie [Griswold]
Daughter of Chauncy & Frances
W. Griswold, Born August 3.
1859, Died March 19, 1879.

We shall all meet on the bright shores
of immortality.

In memory of
350—Sarah A [Keeler]
Daughter of Jonah C, & Henrietta Keeler who Died May 16,
1841 Æ 3 years & 6 mo.

In memory of
351—Charles L. [Keeler]
son of Jonah C & Henrietta
Keeler who died July 5, 1841,
Æ 1 year 7 mo & 17 Days

In memory of
352—Henry [Keeler]
son of Jonah C & Henrietta
Keeler who died July 16, 1842,
Æ 8 months 8 Days

353—Phoebe W, Camp
Born Sept. 18, 1798. Entered
into rest July 15, 1885.

354—Nathan Camp
born May 22 A. D. 1795, died
August 6, 1880.

A just man, he kept the faith to the end

The Grave of

355--*Araty Raymond*
wife of Nathan Camp who
calmly yielded up her spirit to
God April 2. 1846.

Her trust was in Christ and her end was
peace

To the memory of

356--*A. J, Carter,*
a native of New Market E ig-
land Æ, 22 years.

He was drowned in the Mill Pond while
in the employ of Mr Thomas Benedict
Dec. 6, 1834.

J. L.

Sacred to the memory of

357--*Joseph Loris,*
who died Mar 14. AD 1821.
aged 51.

358--*Hezekiah Smith,*
Died June 8, 1852. in his 83 y'r.

Wrapt in the shades of death,
No more that friendly face I see.
Empty ah Empty every place.
Once fil'd so well by thee.

[Granite monument]

359—*William C. Wheeler*
Died July 3, 1889. age 59.

A member of Co. G. 23rd Conn. Vols.
'Twas Hard to give thee up.
But thy will, O God, be done.
Wheeler.

360—*George H. [Roberts]*
son of Nathan & Sarah A. Roberts Died March 25, 1872,
Æ. 17 years 3 Mo's & 8 Days,

He doeth all things well

361—*George B, [Bennett]*
son of George & Mary D. Bennett. Died Dec. 20, 1871, Æ 16
y'rs 11 mo's. & 26 Days

The Lord is my Shepherd

362—*Emily M. [Roberts]*
wife of Wm. O. Roberts. Born
March 19, 1844. Died March 8,
1878.

Mother

In memory of

363--*Betsey Jennings,*
widow of Zalmon Jennings who
died Jan. 29, 1846, aged 73
years & 26 Days.

Dearest mother thou hast left us,
And thy loss we deeply feel
But tis God who has bereft us,
He can all our sorrows heal.

In memory of

364—*Edgar [Clark]*
only son of William & Sally Ann
Clark who died Aug. 9, 1848.
Æ. 23 y'rs & 5 mo.

"Shed not for him the bitter tear,
Nor give the heart to vain regret;
Tis but the Casket that lies here,
The Gem that filled it sparkles yet"

In memory of

365--*Mary Augusta [Clark]*
only daughter of William &
Sally Ann Clark, who died Jan.
1, 1855, Æ. 31 y'rs & 5 mo's.

And art thou gone my darling child.
Oh; art thou, now, no longer mine,
Thou wast to us a season given,
But thy abiding place is heaven.

In memory of

366--*William Clark*
who Died April 8th 1860, aged
65 years 2 mo & 10 Days

But there's a land where death comes not.
Far, Far beyond the tomb;
When on life's waves no more we're tost,
There may we meet the early lost.

In memory of

367--*James E. [St John]*
son of James E. & Mary St.
John who died Nov. 18, 1842.
Æ 2 years & 10 Days

In memory of

368—*Elisha. S. [Clark]*
son of Widow Sarah Clark, who
died Dec. 25, 1828. Æ. 13 years
& 3 mo

Sleep on sweet child and take thy rest.
God call'd thee home when he thought best

Our Mother.

369—*Sarah Clark*
Died at Portchester, N. Y. June
18, 1860, Æ. 67 y'rs. 4 mo's. & 4
D's.

Our mothers gone and soon will we,
Be called to follow on,
We soon will ferry o'er deaths sea,
and meet where mother's gone.

370 - George Frederick [St John]

son of Reuben A. & S. J. St John, died July 6, 1851, Æ 1 y'r 8 mo. & 15 d's.

Our George has gone and left us,
And left this world of vice,
To show the world how fair a flower
Can bloom in Paradise.
Thus sweetly borne, be flies to rest;
We know tis well, nay more tis best,
When we our pilgrims path have trod
O! may we find him with our God!

— :o :—

In memory of

371--Joel Smith

who died Sept. 11, 1853, Æ. 69 y'rs.

In memory of

372—Nancy [Smith]

widow of Joel Smith who died Jan. 16, 1867, Æ 84 y'rs.

373—Melville F, [Raymond]

son of Wm. M. & Sarah E. Raymond Mar, 30, 1854. Æ. 11 m, & 12 d's

It grieved his loving parents sore
With their darling child to part
But think his sufferings now are o'er
Be resigned give God your hearts.
He is not dead but he Melville sleeps
In the gentle Saviours arms
He the little lamb will keep
And protect him now from harm

374--Ruth Eliza [Raymond]

daughter of Wm. M. & Sarah E. Raymond died June 2, 1847, Æ, 3 y'rs, 8 mos. & 22 d's

An early summons Jesus sends
To call a child above—
And whispers o'er the weeping friend
Tis all the fruit of love.

Tis on the Saviours bosom laid,
And feels no sorrow there;
Tis by a heavenly parent fed.
And need no more your care

375 -Sarah Eliza [Raymond]

wife of Wm M Raymond Died March 7, 1882 Æ 65 y'rs, 2 mo's & 18 Days

376—William M. Raymond

Born Jan. 9th, 1809, Died July 5th, 1887.

377—Nellie F,

Her Daughter 1869 1881
[Probably dau of No 378]

378—Phebe A,

wife of Harvey R. Brown. Born Feb. 3, 1810. Died June 20, 1870.

Our Darling Josie

Safe in the arms of Jesus

379—Josephine A, [Raymond]

Daughter of Henry W, & Hannah M Raymond Died Oct 6, 1878, Æ. 7 y's, & 23 D's

380—Ollie [Dann]

son of Charles J, & Jennie E. Dann Died 1879, Æ. 3 years 9 mo's & 15 Days.

Ollie

Suffer little children to come unto me, and of such is the kingdom of Heaven.

Mark

381--Mark H, [Dann]

son of Charles J. & Jennie E. Dann Died April 17, 1891, Æ, 18 years 18 mos. & 13 Days.

We dearly loved our boy
Our love was not in vain
He gave us happiness and joy
Our loss his heavenly gain.

In memory of

382--Burr Smith [Hoyt]

son of Francis & Angenett Hoyt who died Sept. 28, 1853. Æ 27 y'rs 2 mo. & 8 d's

Brother thy name we bless,
Thy providence adore:
Earth has a mortal loss,
Heaven an angel more.

In memory of

383--Susannah Hoyt

wife of Charles Partrick who Died July 20, 1858, aged 29 y'rs 10 mo. & 20 D's.

The grave is now a favored spot
To Saints who sleep in Jesus blessed,
For there the wrecked trouble not
And there the weary are at rest

384--Capt. James T. Johnson

Born July 17, 1819, Died July 19, 1873, aged 54 years & 2 Days.

He has made his last voyage over the sea of life
And cast anchor in a harbor of rest.

384½--Ann M. [Johnson]

wife of Capt. James T. Johnson Died Aug. 16, 1880. aged 57 y'rs 3 ms. & 25 Days.

Our little ones,

385—Harry. [Camp]
Born Jan. 18, 1848. Died Oct. 3,
1849,

Henry
Born July 11, 1849, Died Aug,
15, 1854.
Children of Henry & Anna
Camp.

386—Artie [Fowler]
son of Lewis G & Addie L Fow.
ler Died Mar. 15, 1890, aged 7
years.
"Safe in the arms of Jesus."

387— George S, Raymond
Died May 30, 1886. aged 47 yrs.
6 mos. 27 Ds.

388—Herbert [Hall]
son of Abram D & Ella Hall
Died Feb. 23, 1874, Æ. 4 y'rs 11
mo & 23 D's

Herbbie

389—Emma G. [Sullivan]
Daughter of Joseph & Cordelia
P Sullivan Born June 5, 1847
Died August 18, 1881

390—Cordelia P. Terry,
wife of Joseph Sullivan. Born
Feb. 1st, 1819. Died Nov. 18th,
1883.

A happier lot than ours, and larger
light surrounds thee there.
Mother

391—Maryella Sullivan [Hall]
wife of Abraham D. Hall. Born
Oct. 1st, 1845. Died Nov. 6th,
1883.

Sheltred and safe from sorrow,
Mamma.

392—Susan Isaacs [Hill]
wife of Doctor Asa Hill Died
May 11, 1890.

With the loved ones gone before.

393—Doctor Asa Hill
Died November 26, 1874, aged
59 years.

"He rests from his labors."

394—Rebecca Isaacs,
wife of Charles Isaacs, Died May
31, 1869. aged 72 years.
She sleeps in Jesus.

395—Charles Isaacs,
Died July 18, 1872, aged 77
years

396—George Smith [Hanford]
Died Nov. 12, 1849, aged 11
years 3 mo. & 23 Days.

George Smith
Died March 16, 1836, aged 3
Weeks.

Children of Daniel & Caroline
Hanford,

397—Daniel Hanford
Died Sept. 25. 1857, aged 53 yrs,
9 mo's and 6 Days.

Caroline Smith
His wife Died Mar. 23, 1888,
Æ. 83 yrs and 7 Days.
"He giveth his beloved sleep."

398—Charles E, Hanford
Died May 17, 1883, aged 52 yrs,
& 6 m's,

399—Sarah [Lockwood]
Relict of Stephen Lockwood
(within) was born March 7, 1757.
and ended a life of practical
benevolence, Sept. 21, 1848, aged
91, among her children in Milan,
Ohio, where beneath their joint
memorial repose her remains.

[On the other side of this stone
is seen the following]
In memory of
399½—Capt Stephen Lockwood
who died Feb. 13, 1830, in the
76 year of his age.

400—Sarah Betts
wife of D. Fitch Betts, Died
Nov. 30, 1854, Æ. 57 y'rs 9 mo's
& 6 D's.

[Lays on the ground]

401—Sarah Esther Betts
daughter of Henry & Rebecca
Betts Born March 29, 1804,
Died May 5. 1867

402—Rebecca Betts
widow of Henry Betts Died
Jan. 24. 1851, in the 80th year
of her age.

Henry Betts
Died at Statten Island, N. Y.
Aug. 18. 1815, in the 49th year
of his age.

Died Aug. 31, 1832.

403 —Susan Isaacs, [Betts]
daughter of Daniel F. & Sarah
Betts, Æ. 3 years & 11 months.

404—Uriah Hanford
Died at Unadila, N. Y. Dec 24,
1823, aged 56. years.

Rhoda
His wife Died Aug. 26, 1848,
aged 80, years.

In memory of

405—Franklin, [Hanford]
son of Joseph & Jane Hanford
who died Dec 31, 1843-8, Æ 2
years & 5 mo

In memory of

406—Emma, [Hanford]
Twin Daughter of Joseph P, &
Jane Hanford, who Died Aug.
2, 1850, Æ 7 years & 10 mo.
Of such is the Kingdom of Heaven

In memory of

**407—Phebe Ann, [Jennings
(Hoyt.]**
wife of Henry B, Jennings.
adopted Daughter of Ezra &
Lucretia Hoyt. who Died Feb.
3, 1849, Æ. 26 yrs. 6 mo, & 18
Days.
Precious in the sight of the Lord is the
death of his Saints.—Ps, 116, 15.

In memory of

408—Freddy, [Lockwood]
son of Stephen D & Mary E.
Lockwood, who Departed This
life Jan. 1. 1861, In the 6th year
of His age.

Weep not for little Freddy at home with the
blest
Where the notes of the angels lull him to rest
His lay is now mingled with those in the sky
With those robed in white in glory on high

409—Lucretia [Hoyt]
widow of Ezra Hoyt. Died Oct,
3, 1876. Æ. 86 y'rs & 16 Days.

She sleeps in Jesus

410—Ezra Hoyt,
Died April 23, 1871. Æ. 81 y'rs
8 mos and 6 Days.

Dearest husband thou has left us,
And thy loss we deeply feel;
But tis God who hath bereft us.
He can all our sorrows heal.

[Marble monument]
Brown

411—Addie L, [Brown]
wife of Junius Brown Died
Dec 28, 1887, Æ. 31 yrs. 3 mo's
& 25 Days.
"Blessed are the dead who are in the Lord."

Junius H.
Their son Born Aug. 13, 1886,
Died Oct. 4, 1886
"A bud on earth to bloom in Heaven."

**412 —Abby F. Lobdell [Os-
born]**
wife of Clark H. Osborn. Died
Sept. 20, 1887, aged 67 years.
At Rest.

413— Walter D. [Osborn]
son of C. H. & A F, Osborn
Died Jan. 10, 1879, aged 27
years.
Our loved one

414—Carman Remson
Born Oct. 17, 1822. Died July
14, 1892.

our loved one, Husband
and Father, has gone a
little while before us.

Father
415- *Francis Hoyt*
Died April 27, 1880. Æ. 76 years
2 mo's & 20 Days

Mother

416--*Angenette Smith* [*Hoyt*]
wife of Francis Hoyt D ed June
14, 1886. Æ. 83 years, 2 mos. &
4 Days.

417--*Katie Amelia*, [*Remson*]
Died Sept. 17, 1858, Æ. 2 y'rs
3 mo's & 10 D's.

George Henry
Died Sept. 12. 1858 Æ. 6 w'ks.

Children of Carman & Catherine
A. Remson.

Two little lambs in Heaven,
In the dear Saviour's fold,
Led by a gentle Sheperd,
Where love can ne'er grow cold.

In memory of
418—*Harriet Emily Webb* [*Saunders*]
only daughter of Burr & Law
rinda Saunders, who departed
this life Feb. 21, 1847, Æ. 19
y'rs, & 2 d's

Farewell my dearest Emily farewell
My only daughter dear it was hard
For us to part and when I write these lines
Its with a broken heart, but we did last
Part to meet again in that bright world
Above where Emily and her mother can sing
redeeming love.

Death spares not one! the young the fair
The good the gifted fall;
How rich the harvest gathered there,
Beneath the gloomy pall!

Those who in childhood climbed our knee
And lisped their infant love.
Laid in the silent tomb we see—
The tomb that yawns for more;

419—*Miles Capstick*
Died May 6, 1850. aged 43 years.
"In the cross of Christ I glory."
"Worthy is the Lamb that was slain."

420—*Fanny Capstick*
Died July 19, 1877, aged 74
years.

"At rest in Jesus."

[Double stone]
421--*Mary Ann* [*Capstick*]
Daughter of Miles & Fanny
Capstick Died April 18, 1856.
Æ. 24 years

Miles H. [*Captick*]
son of Miles & Fanny Capstick
Died Aug. 17, 1866. Æ. 29
years.

Another time not—now—will Jesus speak Those
wonderous words he hath in store
Not now but "afterward" will be revealed The
precious fruit of peace and righteous-
ness.

422--*Harriet S. Tryon*
Died July 11, 1884. Æ 49 yrs. &
2 mo's.
Asleep in Jesus.
Tryon

423--*Clarrisse L.* [*Fox*]
wife of William J. Fox. Born
Oct. 23, 1830.

424—*William J. Fox*,
Died Jan 17, 1882, Æ. 52, y'rs 4
m's.
Not d:ad but resting.

425--*Sarah E, Jarvis* [*Christopher*]
wife of Alfred P. Christopher
Died July 26, 1878. Æ. 31 y'rs,
1 mo. & 24 Days,

also infant sons, Isaac Jarvis, &
Robert Edward, Æ. 16 Days.
Loved, Lamented, Blessed.

426--*Isaac P. Jarvis*
Died April 10, 1885, Æ. 73
years & 4 Days.

We thought him faultless,
Knew him to be charitable,
and believed him crowned.

427—*Harriet* [*Jarvis*]
wife of I. P. Jarvis Died April
10, 1855. Æ. 39 y'rs 9 mo's & 10
D's

Also an infant daughter of I. P.
& Harriet Jarvis Died July 7,
1855. Æ. 3 mo's,

428—Mary P. [Jarvis]
died March 3. 1850 Æ. 13 y'rs

How short the race our child has run,
Cut down in all her bloom
The course but yesterday began
Now finish'd in the Tomb.

Mary L.
died Oct. 26, 1851, Æ 1 year & 6
mo's.

Sleep on little one
And take thy rest
God called the home
When he thought best.

Children of Isaac P. & Harriet
Jarvis.

429.Annie Elizabeth Jarvis,
wife of G. W. Nantz. Died Feb.
18, 1866, Æ. 25 y'rs 9 mo's & 21
D's.

A devoted Wife and Kind Mother

Carrie E. Nantz.
Æ. 7 mo's.

A bud on earth, to bloom in Heaven.

430—Caroline [Bennett]
wife of Henry Bennett Died
Jan. 24, 1892, Æ. 73 years, & 5
months,

431—Henry Bennett
Died Sept. 6, 1875. Æ. 6 years &
3 Days

432—William Bennett
Died Sept, 5, 1883. aged 31
years.

433Charles H [Bennett]
son of Henry & Caroline Bennett Died Sept. 16, 1849. Æ 2
y's, 6 mo & 18 d.

Though broken from the parent stem
A bud so sweet and rare,
It blooms on high in fields of light
More lovely fresh and fair

434—Matthew Rawson
Born Dec. 23, 1826. Died May
9, 1882.

INDEX BY NUMBER.

EXPLANATION.

All persons found under each Number are given that Number
in the Index.

Yours Truly

D Hebaut Hoosear

(See Description No. 199.)

Erected by the Children of Lewis Raymond, whose residence was Wilton, Ct.

(See Description No. 230.)

Hon. Thomas Fitch, Colonial Governor of Conn., 1754 to 1766.

(See Description No. 83.)

A VIEW OF EAST NORWALK CEMETERY AS SEEN FROM THE EAST ENTRANCE DOOR OF THE M. E. CHURCH, IN THAT PLACE.

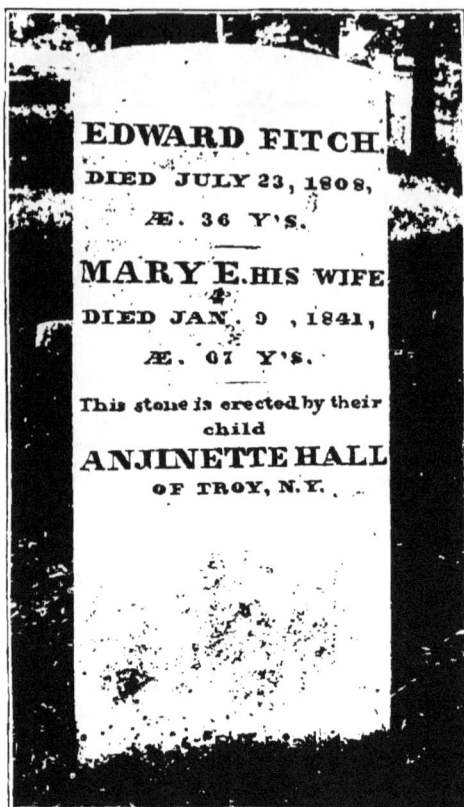

EDWARD FITCH.
DIED JULY 23, 1808,
Æ. 36 Y'S.

MARY E. HIS WIFE
DIED JAN. 9, 1841,
Æ. 07 Y'S.

This stone is erected by their
child
ANJINETTE HALL
OF TROY, N. Y.

(See Description No. 238.)